Woman in Black

Selected Poems
By Roger Adams

In Memory of Anne
08.01.1938 - 20.11.2007

Published by

A Roger Adams Original

Printed By
Cambrian Printers

Illustrated by
Roger Adams

ISBN: 978-0-9559631-1-7

2008

Woman in Black

Contents

Introduction	1
A Rose by Any Other Name	2
Pictures of Anne	3
Yes Dear. I know Dear	4
Woman in Black	5
Anne	6
Dreamland	7
The Writing of True Love	8
True Love	9
Bora Bora	10
The Courtesan's Embrace	12
Fluttering Wings	13
Shall We Dance?	14
Now that Anne has Gone	15
Seychelles Surf	16
A Moment in Time	17
The Age of Reason	18
Love at First Sight	19
Examined	20
Banned	21
The Kingfisher	22
Interlude	23
The Otter	24
Jack Russells	25
The Healing Power of Cats	26
The Little Black Cat	27
Lloyd Webber	28
Therapy	29
A 3 O'Clock in the Morning Thing	30
Landfill	31
Compost	32

A Thank You to Linda and Affen	33
Wallflowers	34
Mallard	35
The Swan	36
Reptilian Scales	37
Dawn	38
Service with a Smile	39
The Drunk	40
A Desert Island Disc	41
Anne's Legacy	42
Be My Valentine	43
Fishing	44
Sex and the Colour Green	45
The Cellar Bar	46
Cellar Bar Girl	47
Respect	48
Pain	49
A Poem for This Day	50
A Universal Vision	52
On the Way to Somewhere Else	53
Introspection	54
The River Siedi	55
The Heron	56
The Psychiatrist's Chair	57
White Vans	58
Anne's Father Jack	59
Global Village	60
Age Concern : Extreme Makeover	61
Quality of Life	62
A Cat Called Angharad	63
The Beauties of Aberystwyth	64
Thank You	

INTRODUCTION

This volume is unashamedly a tribute to my late wife Anne. She was my muse and my inspiration for everything I have done. Is this yet another ego-trip? Yes. The printers tell me it is known as Vanity Publishing. However, at seventy-one you are allowed such flights of fancy and modern technology has made vulgar indulgences so much more accessible. Most of the poems in this book were written to amuse Anne or to show her how much I loved her. We were married for forty-five years and I count myself the luckiest man on earth that she loved me and chose to spend the rest of her life with me. Even though 'Cellar Bar Girl' indicates a deep appreciation of the beauty of other women, I can still feel Anne's arm linking tightly with mine as she snuggles up chuckling away at the sheer temerity of my thoughts.

I have found poetry to be a wonderful way of saying thank you to friends and acquaintances and I am fortunate that the lines inspired by their kindnesses burst into my brain and on to the page, usually at 4am the following morning, so that my response is aptly prompt.

At other times the inspiration anticipates an event. When I was faced with being the host and conducting the ceremony at Anne's Cremation Service, I was particularly worried. However, two days before that fateful day, the poem 'Anne' came to my aid and provided me with the 'sermon' to fit the occasion. It helped me to get through without cracking up before I pressed the button on the lectern which closed the curtains as we all bade her farewell.

I hope there is sufficient humour in these pages to balance the tragic emotions I have penned here. I hope also that those of you who have suffered similar times of such loss will gain some comfort and see in these lines moments that reflect your individual experiences.

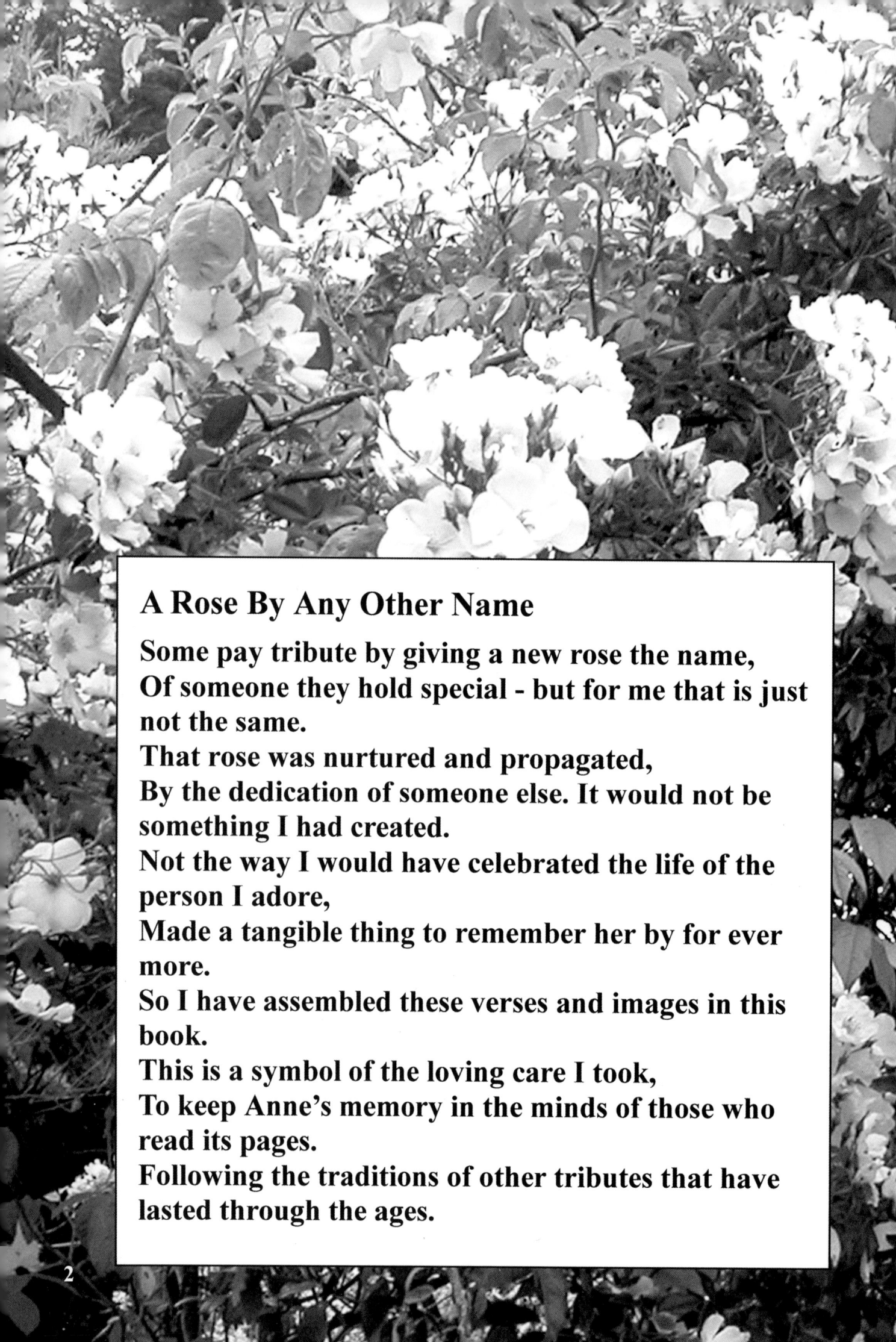

A Rose By Any Other Name

Some pay tribute by giving a new rose the name,
Of someone they hold special - but for me that is just not the same.
That rose was nurtured and propagated,
By the dedication of someone else. It would not be something I had created.
Not the way I would have celebrated the life of the person I adore,
Made a tangible thing to remember her by for ever more.
So I have assembled these verses and images in this book.
This is a symbol of the loving care I took,
To keep Anne's memory in the minds of those who read its pages.
Following the traditions of other tributes that have lasted through the ages.

Pictures of Anne

Anne was always impeccably groomed and elegantly dressed, yet of vanity there was no trace.
She tended to frown on having pictures of herself displayed around the place.
Most of the images, therefore, remained hidden and virtually forgotten,
That was until her untimely death, when,
Rediscovered, I found in them great comfort and solace.
How I loved her, her inner beauty, her lovely face.

'Yes Dear. I Know Dear.'

My Darling Roger,

Ever since I first met you, you have been the only one for me,
But look at my expression in this picture, you're an intelligent man, can't you see,
How embarrassed I am feeling, you can really be an awful pain,
When I see that you've got that infernal camera out again.
I know you think that I am beautiful, I really am quite flattered,
But if you showed these pictures to our friends you know that I'd be shattered.
You must realise by now, I do my best to ruin every shot,
By frowning or talking, a photographer's model I certainly am not!
I know, to catch me unaware, you resort to devious ways,
But please believe me, I do not relish being subjected to the public's gaze.
I love your dedication. The perseverance that you've got,
But if I had my way, I would scrap the lot.
I realise I am not here now to stop you publishing this book.
Please, be discreet, be sensible, I understand the loving care it took.
After all these years, knowing you, it does not matter what I say,
I know that you are going to do it anyway.
Whatever it is that you eventually decide to do,
Nothing will stop me from always loving you.

All my Love,
Anne

Woman in Black

Enigmatic and erotic image pictured on the wall.
Reveal to me the secret of it all.
Disclose the source of your all-conquering powers,
That hold me captive here for hours.
Woman in Black – woman of mystery,
Dark shades conceal the look in your eyes from me.
Are you the girl I once knew or a complete stranger?
Behind those impenetrable glasses, intrigue and danger?
Lips that are provocative and pouting,
Full and deep red, voluptuous and tempting.
Lips demanding to be kissed.
Skin crying out to be caressed.
Velvet, soft, white and so alluring.
That face so magical and utterly entrancing.
Your ability to surprise me, never ceases to amaze.
Casting me under the spell of your bewitching ways.

Anne

As an artist I know that a few brush strokes can portray a face,
And the human eye will fill in all the vacant space.
So if you loved a girl as I loved Anne,
It is quite possible that her vision in my eyes can,
Have ignored a blemish, conveyed only what I wanted to see,
The beauty that she was to me.
But this is clearly not the case,
All of you who met her, knew that face.
What always amazed me was that she was quite unaware,
Of her lovliness, she did not seem to care.
She did not use that beauty, she had no vice,
Although she may have used it as a device,
Over the course of many years,
To seductively convert me to her ideas.
When I first met her, captivated by her vivacity,
Bright, flashing eyes, her vibrant energy.
And as our love over time endured,
Her loveliness intensified as it matured.
Was it luck that brought us together or was it fate?
That I was blessed to have her as my devoted mate.
A posting to St Athan paved the way,
A telephone call from Marina just to say,
There was a party at the Royal Infirmary.
How could I know how vital that invitation would be to me.
A glance across the room - a vision met my eye,
A navy blue polka dotted dress seemed to float by.
Time came to a stop. It was love at first sight.
There and then I vowed with all of my might,
I must seize this momentous opportunity.
Anne was the only girl for me.

18.11.07

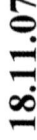

Dreamland

As I make my way to a lonely bed,
Visions of Anne invade my head.
A rendezvous in Dreamland there to keep,
As I drift off, deep into sleep.
The sensation of her presence is so real,
I am overwhelmed by the emotion I feel.
I reach beside me but her lovely body is not there.
I am driven to the limits of despair.
So many images of her beauty in my memory,
Alternate pangs of love and torment haunt my reverie.

06.04.08

Writing True Love

I wrote the next poem when we were on board QE2 in the middle of the Atlantic Ocean on our way to the Caribbean. I awoke at 0500 on 29th November 2003 with the idea for this poem. I sat in the lounge of our suite, while Anne was still fast asleep, and the words just cascaded on to the page. It was two days before our 41st Wedding Anniversary and I am convinced that somewhere in my subconscious, my brain had been beavering away and early on this morning it decided that it was time to download. I have no idea how it happens, I am just glad that it does.

I made a card for Anne and on the 1st December when we dined with Alan and Norma Bye, I recited the poem at the table whilst holding Anne's hand. This was not so much an act of endearment , rather a precaution to stop Anne from hitting me.

I read this poem in my address at the Celebration of Anne's Life and I asked the guests to listen with a smile on their faces. You can often tell as much about the writer of a poem as the subject and I suppose I don't come out of it too well. In a way it epitomises our relationship. A girl who still loves to bits the writer of those lines has to be very special indeed.

True Love

I love the bags beneath your eyes,
I love the cellulite around your thighs,
The infectious laugh, that lovely smile,
Your courage, your inimitable style.

I love the scars from the surgeon's knife,
The way you've fought adversity all your life,
The way you've stuck with me through thick and thin.
Your tolerance of all my faults. Where shall I begin?

I love your figure when you breathe in.
I love your warmth when you've been drinking gin.
I love your legs when you wear high heels.
The way the touch of your soft lips feels.

I love your arms though you prefer to cover them with sleeves.
I love the scent your presence leaves.
I love your derrière, compact and round.
Your accent. Its Welsh tone's seductive sound.

I love the way you captivate our friends.
After disagreements, the way we make amends.
The way you let me think I'm always right.
The reassuring way you hold me tight.

I love you stubborn, I love when you forget.
I loved you from the moment we first met.
I love all these things because they are you.
A love that will be for ever true.

29.11.03

Bora Bora

Bora Bora. The ultimate tropical paradise of idyllic far off places.
You've seen the brochures with the beautiful people that fill the pages?
Well that was us. Anne was lovely and in her prime.
It was such a phenomenal time.
And every picture that I took,
Had that glossy magazine look.
It really was the perfect place,
To match the beauty of Anne's figure and her face.
Her velvet skin and legs so slender,
Had the darkest tan I can remember.
She was sparkling, free, wild in a native splendour,
I wished we could have stayed there forever.
A time of wonderful memories to savour.
Bloody Mary. Not the amply bosomed red hot mamma in South Pacific,
But a long-house restaurant that was utterly fantastic!
Sandy floors, palm tree stumps to seat,
The diners there sat down to eat,
Barbecued seafood, partake of fine French wines.
Hula Hula dancers in casual lines.
They were not a glossy troupe but locals of all shapes size and age,
With natural rhythm. So graceful as they filled the rustic stage.
They swayed in their dance with garlands and grass skirt,
Their shuffling feet stirring the sandy dirt.
And that walk back with the one I love.
Complete darkness save for a pathway of stars above.
A milky way leading us directly back to our hotel.
Such a romantic tale I have to tell.
Parting the black, palm silhouette of lofty trees,
Waving gently to the prompting of a tropic breeze.
Anne hugging me close, frightened by the sound,
Of land crabs scuttling in the plantations all around.
Surf breaking on a distant reef beyond the lagoon.
Why did it have to end so soon?

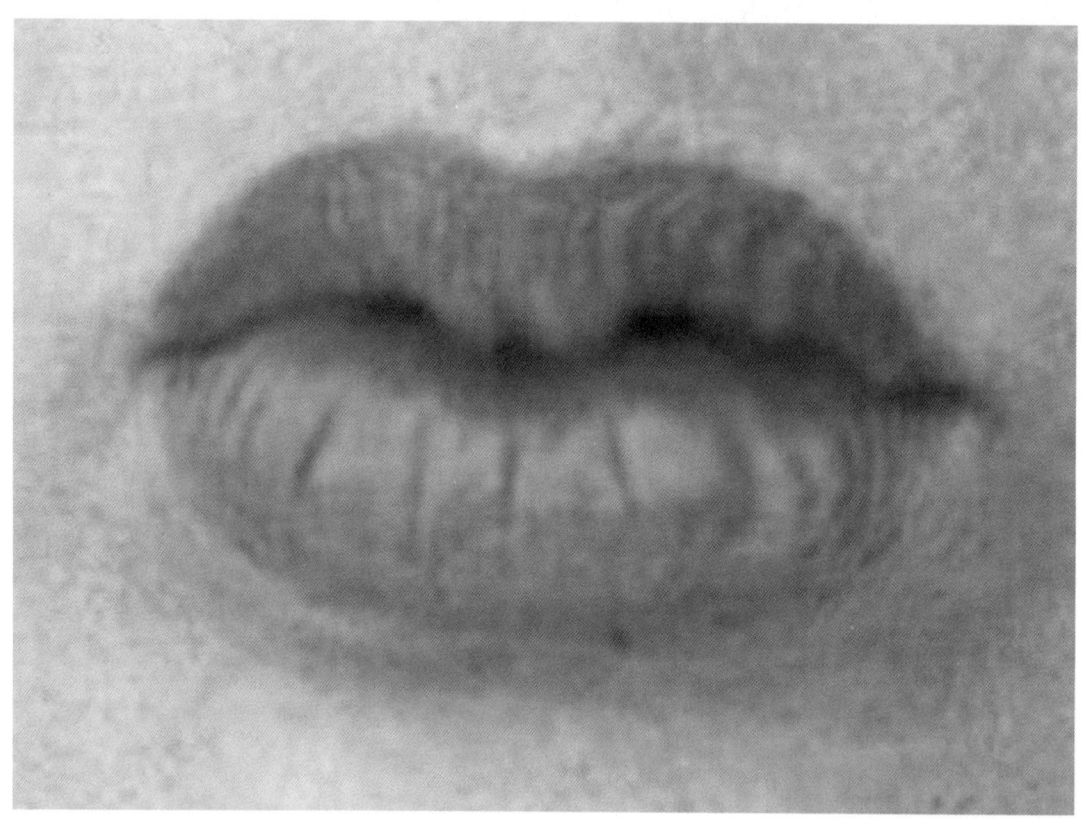

The Courtesan's Embrace

Your sensuous bow of crimson lips,
Moist with your aphrodisiac nectar drips,
To anoint the speeding arrow tips,
That penetrate deep in my heart,
Even the most resolute defence will fall apart.
With swelling desire that drives the start,
Of my succumbing to your wanton sexual advance,
Transfixed in your bewitching trance,
Writhing together in a wild fandango dance.
The timeless moment of our embrace,
That stimulates my pulse to race,
As I surrender completely to your beautiful face.
Captivated by the clasp of your encircling thighs,
Elated by the climax of your moans and sighs,
Drowning in the deep twin pools of your seductive eyes.
20.10.07

Fluttering Wings

My love for you is deep and never ending,
As the fluttering of wings of birds ascending.
Reaching heights where lungs and heart are bursting,
Seeking the oxygen of your love for which my soul is thirsting.
Breaking through the mists to blinding light,
Dispelling the dark shadows of the night.
You are my muse, my inspiration and my lover.
The great beauty of my life – devoted mother.
You are my temptress, my seducer and my concubine.
My eyes adore the curve of breast and hips – that classic line.
Now that you have been restored to me,
Let us enjoy the triumph of your recovery.

10.09.07

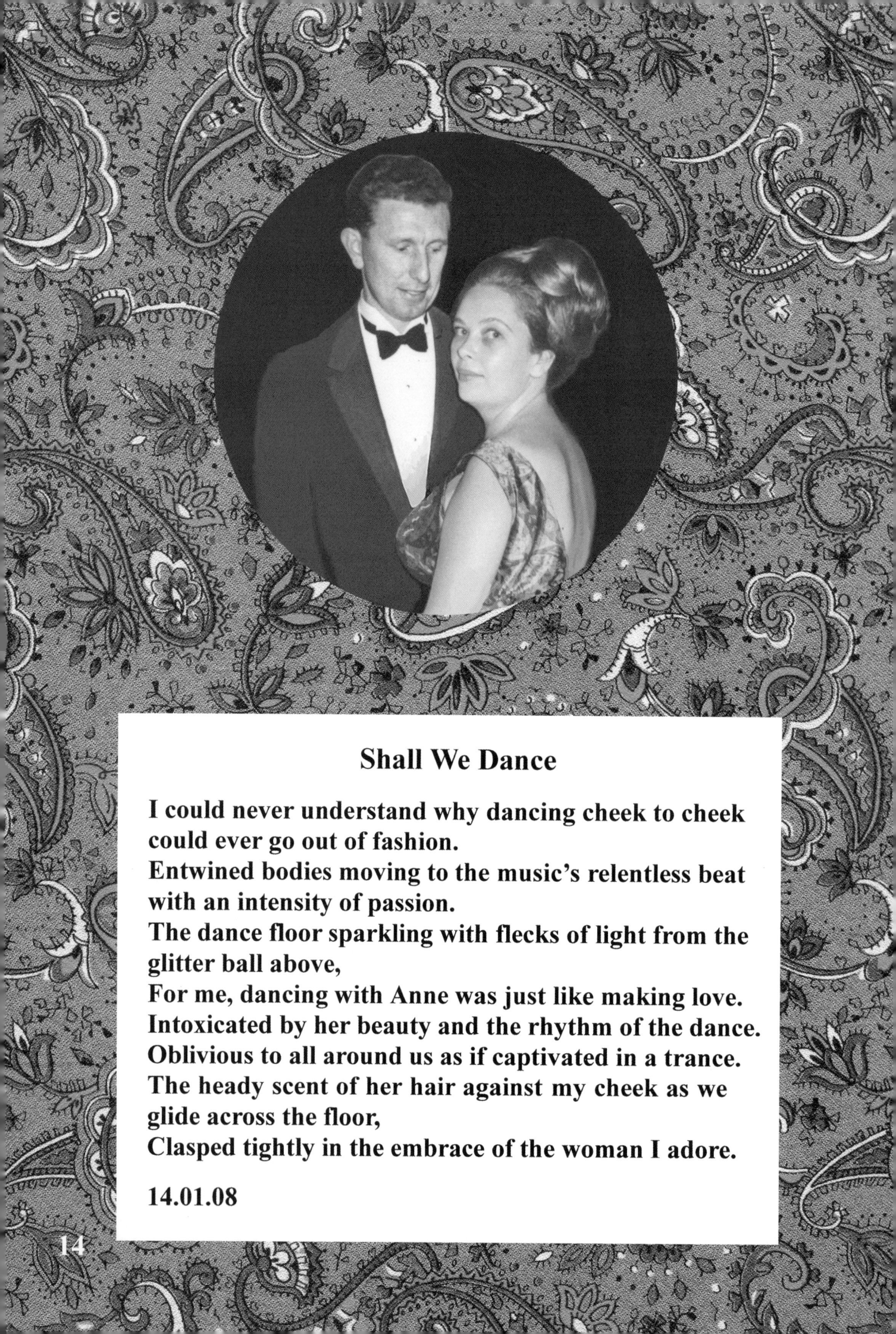

Shall We Dance

I could never understand why dancing cheek to cheek could ever go out of fashion.
Entwined bodies moving to the music's relentless beat with an intensity of passion.
The dance floor sparkling with flecks of light from the glitter ball above,
For me, dancing with Anne was just like making love.
Intoxicated by her beauty and the rhythm of the dance.
Oblivious to all around us as if captivated in a trance.
The heady scent of her hair against my cheek as we glide across the floor,
Clasped tightly in the embrace of the woman I adore.

14.01.08

Now That Anne Has Gone

When Death, suddenly steals away the one that you adore,
Leaving you empty and lost for ever more,
That treasured image of her, lovely and sublime,
Is of her when she was in her prime.
Not sullied by debilitating disease or grave impediment,
No morbid regrets and deeply saddened sentiment.
Still absolutely gorgeous, how I loved her so.
She was my Princess Diana, my Marilyn Monroe.
I will fill the house with pictures to remind me of her at every turn,
How my deep passion for her would smoulder and burn..
A fire that is still as intense as when we first met,
Now eats away deep inside me - and yet,
If only just once more to kiss those lips - I wish. Oh how I wish.
But Death cannot steal away the memories of Anne I cherish.

She was my wise counsel, my guiding light.
The benign influence that ensured whatever I did was right.
I now realise that all I ever did was for her approval.
When I failed she was there to see me through it all.
But if my failure was for my lack of courage or dedication,
I knew I risked losing her respect - risked her condemnation.
I suppose it was plain for all to see,
Having both her love and her respect was everything to me.

12.01.08

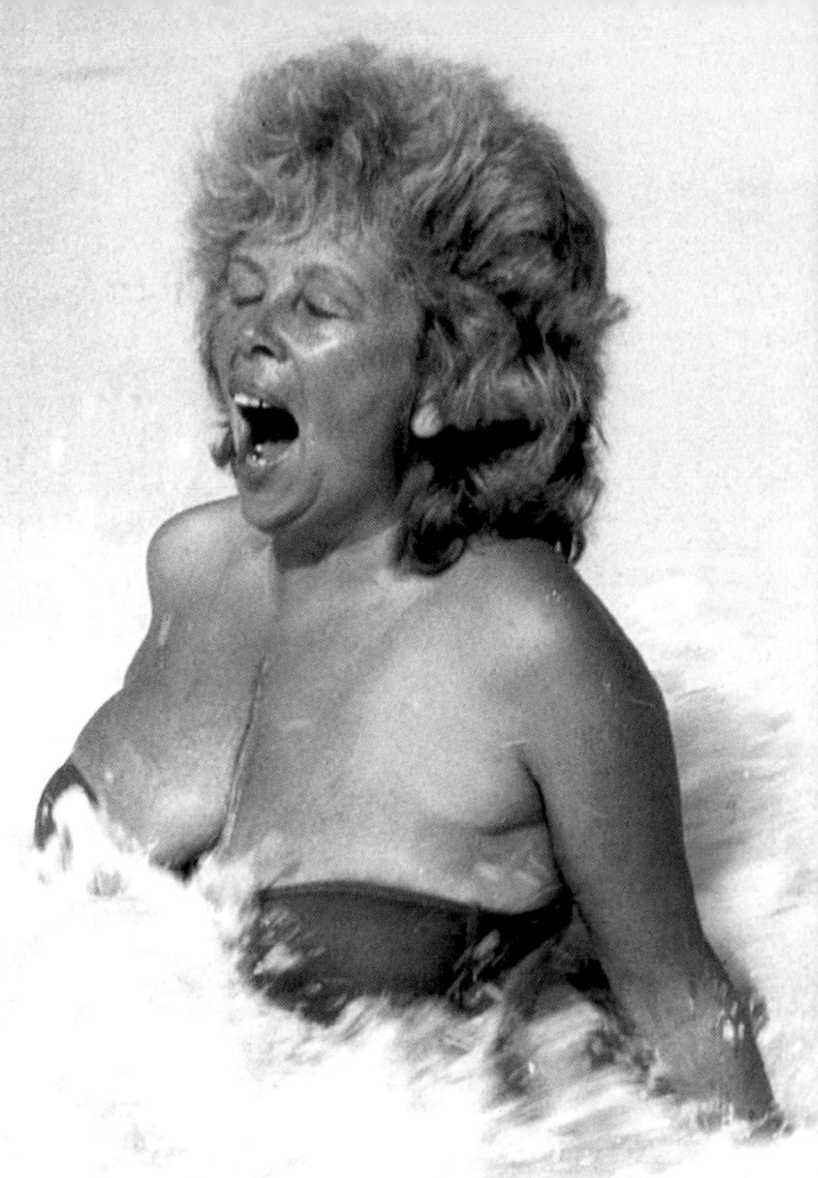

Seychelles Surf

Anne was in her fiftieth year,
We had not flown abroad recently for fear,
That it was too soon after her first heart operation,
This was an exciting time of liberation.
She had stopped smoking and had put on weight,
But she was still gorgeous, she looked absolutely great!
We were in the Seychelles on holiday,
At the Hotel Europa for a three week stay.
We visited Brendan Grimshaw, a retired Editor of the Times,
Who had bought Moyenne Island to live in sunnier climes,
In the Marine Reserve on this tiny speck of land.
A pyramidal rock surrounded by its halo of white sand.
We clambered down a narrow path to reach,
This quiet little cove with its deserted beach.
I was completely entranced by the sight,
Of Anne playing in the surf - the sheer delight,
That shone so brightly in her face,
As she enjoyed these moments in such an exotic place.

A Moment in Time

When bereavement forces you to floods of tears,
It's amazing how one's brain can flash back some forty years,
Effortlessly spanning time to find,
An isolated moment deep in the mind.
It was August in 1966, we had returned from Singapore.
We were staying with my parents in Epping just before,
I took up my new Fighter Command post at Bentley Priory.
We were walking along Epping High Street past the Library,
On a warm summer's day in the company of my father.
The twins were being looked after by my mother.
I had bumped in to an old school friend and was catching up behind,
Anne and my father had continued. This was the image in my mind.
She wore a tight top, sage green leggings and stilettos with a carefree air,
All this topped with her magnificent mane of red tinged hair.
At that time, stretch material using lycra was still quite new.
The fabric hugged Anne's figure, every curve clearly on view.
I suddenly became aware of the backward glances of the passersby.
Even women took a second look at her, with an envious eye.
When you walk alongside someone as beautiful as Anne,
You are unaware of this, but now quite plainly you can,
Observe the reaction to her wholesome beauty.
It made me realise even more just how lucky,
I was to have her as my wife,
This gorgeous creature, the love of my life.

The Age of Reason
(A Poem to my Wife)

Now that I have reached my seventieth year,
Of growing old I hold no fear,
I might wear a chunky gold medallion and purple flares,
Dye and perm the remains of my receding hairs.
However I am certain you would not be impressed,
By the outlandish way that I am dressed.
I celebrate my few successes and rue my many failures too,
I am grateful for my marriage, my children and my love for you.
I may not have attained the highest rank,
But I've had an interesting life and for that I have to thank,
My parents and the role models of my formative years.
The Arthur Garwells and Buster Cockings, the teachers I must have driven near to tears.
That they persevered has stood me in good stead,
They managed to hammer some semblance of reason in my head.
However forcefully one might attempt to thrust,
A fist into a bucket of water, sadly one must,
Accept that when the limb is removed now dripping wet,
The water level still turbulent as yet,
Eventually returns to its original status quo,
That the hand ever intruded no-one will ever know.
So in life there can be little if anything left to show,
Perhaps a faint and subtle afterglow.
14.06.06

The inspiration for this verse was one of Anne's favourite poems 'When I Grow Old I will Wear Purple' by Jenny Joseph written in 1932.

Love at First Sight

That I should see you floating in that polka dot dress vivacious spirit,
That I should love you deeply and always from that very minute,
Oblivious to all other sounds save for your sparkling voice,
Knowing with such certainty that you would be my choice.

Despite the family torment across the religious divide,
We chose to travel life's path side by side.
To lose you now would be for me a devastating end,
Too awful, too terrible for me to comprehend.

16.09.03

EXAMINED

At the Prince Philip Hospital, Llanelli we spent most of the day.
To the Pre-Assessment Unit ,in a Portakabin, we made our way.
My induction appointment prior to a hip replacement,
Was the reason for my visiting this most modern establishment.
I was scanned, swabbed - had blood and samples taken in the nicest possible way.
I listened intently to what the general and orthopaedic nurses had to say,
We had lunch in the canteen so that I could produced the where-with-all to test.
I cannot instantly oblige even when I am at my best.
Then to Pathology and Radiology for further examination.
Lying on the couch, exposed yet again, to lethal radiation.
If ever I was to attempt to sow wild oats - no thanks!
I am fully convinced that I would now be firing blanks!
I was examined by a beautiful, petite and curvaceous clinician.
I was required to drop my trousers and adopt a certain position.
Just in case by some remote possibility I strayed,
I was accompanied by 'she who must be obeyed'.
This vision, the Doctor, complete with stethoscope accessory,
Explained the consequences of the operation and what was necessary,
If I was to take advantage of this prosthesis and make a full recovery.
She asked if I had ever experienced palpitations.
"Only with beautiful women in close encounter situations",
She then revealed that I now suffered from defibrillation.
Like a prestigious award she bestowed on me this new affliction.
I had joined the hallowed ranks of ex-presidents and our own Prime Minister.
I did not find this breaking news in any way remotely sinister.
At my age this could hardly come as a surprise.
After all, she was not warning of my imminent demise.
At last my whole life now seemed to have been worthwhile.
I wore this new status like a badge with a swagger and a smile.
I have been extra-ordinarily lucky - I am not used to being ill,
Compared to Anne, who has had more than her fill,
Of open heart surgery and related problems that such trauma entails.
It seems ironic that I should now be the one to go off the rails.

12.09.06

Banned

Subjected to extreme torture by the physio-terrorist.
Yet all the aches and pains continue to persist!
Then visited by my occupational therapist,
Who issued me a weighty instruction list.
That I read it and commit to memory she did insist,
If I was to make a full recovery,
From my recent hip replacement surgery.
I studied this draconian set of rules.
I was issued with an intriguing kit of tools.
A long yellow shoe horn and a helping hand,
Two walking sticks to help me to stand.
No driving for six weeks the leaflet said!
No sex for three months the instructions read!
Now denied the two main interests in a modern man's life,
I was even betrayed by my once loyal wife!
I was now banned from the open road.
Confined within the four walls of my abode.
A psychological trauma both fundamental and complex.
Banned from driving and forbidden to have sex!
This was not part of the strategic plan,
When I agreed to become a bionic man.
Denied these pleasures, what was I to do with myself?
Literally stranded on the proverbial shelf.
Legs dangling like a raggedy doll above the ground,
Abandoned in the 'Lost & Found'.
I wondered how I would cope.
Would I have to sit around and mope?
Surely this was too much to bear,
Driven to the outer limits of despair.
Would this sustained period of abstinence,
Lead to a permanent state of impotence?
What would happen to my equipment by which I set great store?
Would I forget what it was for?
Despite all this I have to stress,
I had been so well looked after by the NHS.
Receiving treatment worth several thousand pounds to me,
Delivered at the 'point of contact' absolutely free!

21.11.06

The Kingfisher

When autumn storms bring on torrential rain,
The Teifi and the Siedi are running high again,
The streams, now turbulent and muddied make,
The kingfisher come to fish the clear water of our lake.

The ruffled green and azure feathers of its crest,
Dark pointed beak and ruddy breast,
It rides its perch buffeted by the breeze,
Beneath the surface, tiny fish it sees.

I first saw a kingfisher on the river Bure,
Sailing the Norfolk Broads - childhood memories still endure,
That neon flash of blue - the bird disturbed,
A fleeting glance was all that I observed.

Now fifty years later living among Welsh hills,
Once again sight of this bird the 'twitcher' thrills,
Perched on a weeping willow early in the day,
Plunging beneath the surface to capture its prey.

Now undisturbed it can be clearly seen,
From the windows of the house, it has been,
A source of great enjoyment and delight,
To watch for hours such a fantastic sight.

Despite all this, it causes me concern,
That this elusive bird should have to turn,
To local ponds and lakes to stay alive,
We must do all we can to help these rare creatures to survive.

16.08.02

INTERLUDE

I would like to take this opportunity to thank my many friends and soul-mates who have helped me get some meaning back into my life. Several are, of course, the subject of poems in this volume.

To Gary, for instance, who suggested that I go to the Cellar Bar to perform my poetry. One of the simplest but best pieces of advice I have ever had.

Monica, Anne's cousin, who writes charming poetry and short stories herself, has been a constant encouragement to me in moving forward. I thank her also for her reassurance with the concept of this volume.

I thank Annette Ecuyere Lee for generously giving her time to explain all about self-publishing.

To Steve and April who have created the institution that is the Cellar Bar. Long may it prosper.

To Simone Mansell Broome for establishing a poetry tradition there that is genuine and openly welcoming to anyone who wishes to take part or just enjoy poetry.

To Dai Jones and everyone at Cambrian Printers who made the production of this book such an interesting and pleasant experience. To them this is not just another print order. They are very much a part of the creative process and I value their help and advice.

The wise advice is that you will never make money out of poetry unless you are one of the Seamus Heaneys of this world. I will probably give most of the copies of this book away to my friends anyway. Making money is not the point. Firstly, it is a tribute to Anne and secondly I believe in the principle that it is never too late to break new ground and meet new people who become lifelong friends. For that reason I thank everyone who has made this possible.

The Otter

Once hunted near to extinction with dog and gun,
How could man persecute a creature so full of fun?
They splash, twist and tumble as they play,
Yet can swim past undetected in the middle of the day.

A sleek body, three feet long,
A powerful tail, tapered and strong,
And webbed feet, attributes by which they obtain,
Such speed and agility in their watery domain.

An otter can swim under water for a quarter of a mile,
Large lungs help it stay submerged up to four minutes while,
It overturns stones and searches for its prey.
It consumes up to three pounds of small fish every day.

Sighting an otter is still quite rare,
Nevertheless the signs of its activity are there,
Fish bones and scales and oily spraints are found,
Left in prominent places to mark out its ground.

To find an Otter holt look for water undisturbed and quiet,
Where trees and dense undergrowth hide it from sight.
Secure in a bank-side hole above the flood water mark,
Hollowed out to make its den there safe and dark.

They eat mostly coarse fish up to six inches in length,
They rarely trouble trout and salmon that have the strength,
To swim fast enough so that they can outpace,
The agility of the otter and escape its predatory chase.

The casual observer will rarely catch a glimpse,
Of these secretive creatures that will elude any attempts,
Of all but the most patient who devote time throughout the year,
In hours of silent vigil to await the moment they appear.

The outlook for the otter at last appears more secure,
As conservationists, land owners and farmers now ensure,
Territories are protected and habitats are restored,
Indeed, actions that all nature lovers should applaud.

19.01.03

Jack Russells

(A little doggerel about little dogs)

Bramble

I rely on your discretion, my wife is completely unaware,
For the past three years I have been having an affair.
She is petite and flirtatious, answers to the name of Bramble,
This diminutive, little black and white Jack Russell.

When she was young and tiny, she was particularly sweet,
Fussing around me and getting under my feet.
I nearly trod on her - it really made me wince.
The strange thing is, this little dog has loved me ever since.

She lives at Henfryn Farm with Rob McCall, her other man.
I do my best to visit her as often as I can.
She's always there to greet me with a chewed-up ball or sock.
For a cat person like me, this has come as quite a shock.

It was so sad to learn of Chalky's recent fate.
That famous TV star - Rick Stein's devoted mate.
He had his own TV series, Anne and I were loyal fans,
In which this balding fellow mucked about with pots and pans.

We watched, fascinated as the camera followed on his travels,
Chasing mice and rabbits in fields of vegetables.
Touring the whole country on his single-minded quest,
Seeking out producers of food that was the very best.

I summon you to raise your glasses. Let us drink a toast!
They may be very small but they are the dogs I love the most.
They are all great characters and loyal to the end.
Let us all pay a tribute to mankind's best friend!

The Healing Power of Cats

I have this foolishly romantic notion,
That when cats bestow on you their affection,
When they rub themselves against you and loudly purr,
They mysteriously and magically transfer,
Some of their good fortune, maybe a life or two,
This is their selfless gift to you.
Once the witch's dark familiar,
When they practiced the art of Wicca,
The black cat knew all their pagan ways,
In those far off medieval days.
Burned at the stake, their healing knowledge lost,
In the name of religion at such a terrible cost.
A cat's instinct retains a deep seated memory,
Defying the turbulent acts of history.
These independent creatures have the power, if you believe,
To heal sorrow and woes, your aches and pains relieve.

The Little Black Cat

There was a cat for whom I had a great affection,
This was not a distant recollection,
It all happened comparatively recently,
She used to visit us quite regularly.
No house cat, she lived next door by the outhouse in a shed.
It was our neighbours by whom she was fed.
She did not come in search of food,
Although I'm certain that she could,
Have found a juicy field mouse for a meal.
This could not be the reason for the appeal,
Of padding across to say hello,
And join me to look at the garden below.
I was just grateful that she came,
I did not even know her name.
Completely black with a stumpy tail,
I valued the friendship of this diminutive female.
She'd jump up on the bench beside me,
Rubbing her head against my knee,
Then she would sit erect and share the view,
The way that all good friends should do.
The moral of the story? The affection that she offered,
Was never given because a bribe of food was proffered.
It was quite genuine and pure,
A sweet memory that will endure.

Lloyd Webber

Dear David & Tara,

**It occurred to me that it was extraordinarily unfair,
That for the concert you had sponsored there was no chance of being there.
Morgan's Brasserie and Time wait for no man it has been said,
At the Festival's busiest period one must earn one's daily bread.
I ordered a Julian Lloyd Webber disc online but sadly must advise,
An Email in reply announced the news of its demise.
They are out of stock with no plans to re-issue,
I confess I wiped away a tear with a handy Kleenex tissue.
However, Julian was not the only Lloyd Webber in the pack,
He and his brother Andrew had decided that they would back,
A production of their father's works which I commend to you,
Please accept this CD called Invocation for you to listen to.
03.09.07**

A Thank you card to Tara and David - Morgan's Brasserie.

Therapy   A Poem to Geoff and Jane

If you were to kiss my cheeks you would taste the salt of tears,
Streaming down my face - recalling the years,
Of deep and constant love that now are lost.
Anne has gone, leaving me to count the cost,
In happiness and humour, warmth and beauty,
Wisdom, common-sense and the sheer purity,
Of heart that made her all I ever wanted.
Now I am an empty shell - broken and demented.
Now I have to rethink my life.
Now afflicted by the passing of my lovely wife.
When personal tragedy strikes, nothing can relieve the pain,
But if by good fortune you have friends like Geoff and Jane,
Who take you in and administer their brand of pet therapy,
Buster, Merlin and Jasper the dogs and cats Claude and Tibby,
You cannot fail to raise a smile,
As these sweet animals in their special way beguile,
You with their foibles, romping to and fro,
Capturing your heart as if deep down they know,
That you are hurting to your very core,
Barely able to bear the heart ache any more.
An early morning spin to moor-land hills.
Crisp and bright blue skies dispel the ills,
And sorrow that have beset you,
When at a loss to know what best to do.
Intellectual conversation demands the need to think,
Dragging you back from the very brink.
A warm log-fired room, a hearty meal.
Hospitality that soothes the hurt you feel.
I thank you both for the unique and touching way,
You administered your brand of therapy yesterday.

A 3'Oclock in the Morning Thing

It happens quite often in the middle of the night, I get a new idea.
If I don't get up and write it down, I always have this fear,
That by the time that morning comes, I am certain to find,
Every last detail has vanished from my mind.

I really do not know why this regularly occurs,
That I should suddenly awake with this urge to write some verse.
I find it quite unnerving, the strange workings of my brain,
The thing is, it happens to me time and time again.

It's as if the old grey cells have been working overtime,
Deep in my subconscious, composing some complicated rhyme.
Why should they go ballistic in the middle of the night?
When most sensible people are asleep and tucked up tight.

My brain decides to download this brand new composition,
It has by now become something of a tradition.
This must be the oddest thing that you have ever heard,
But when I read it through, I rarely have to change a word.

02.03.07

Landfill

We really ought to find a much better way,
To dispose of the rubbish we generate each and every day.
Landfill sites often have quaint and ironic names you'll find.
Silent Valley and High Heaven are examples that come to mind.
The reason is that very few people venture there,
They avoid the awful stench that saturates the air.
The rotting source of methane, the source of illness and disease,
Spread by flocks of seagulls that fly in on the breeze.
To scavenge and pick over the stuff we do not want.
To these birds and other carrion it's a fast food restaurant.
It only takes a little time, just a little thought,
That when we dispose of rubbish we should all attempt to sort,
It into different categories, paper, cans, glass and plastic.
So that it is easy to recycle. It should not be that fantastic!
Don't buy expensive compost, make your own from kitchen waste.
Use it for home-grown vegetables. Enjoy that special taste.
If all this unwanted rubbish was treated as a valuable resource,
Recycling could save on raw materials and money too of course.

Compost

I have got this composting lark down to a fine art.
In saving the planet I play my part.
I do not include pernicious weeds,
Which, when dispensing compost, spread their seeds.
Each year I produce 2 cubic metres or more,
A bank of four large bins provides the means to store,
Kitchen scraps, shredded paper and miscellaneous garden waste,
This is not a process that can be achieved in haste.
Patience of course brings its reward,
And within 6 or 7 months you can afford,
To use this compost to mulch each and every flower bed,
Thus conserving moisture, so experts have said.
Dealing with vast amounts of grass cuttings is not easy,
It tends to make the compost acid and greasy.
I leave them to dry out and decompose,
In a sheltered spot alongside one of my hedgerows.
This material becomes quite peaty after a while,
And adds some bulk to the decomposing pile.
The population of thin red worms break down the soil,
The field mice nesting in the heap save me the toil,
Of turning over tons of enriched matter,
Until it's time for me to scatter,
This valuable product to stimulate new growth and fertility,
And make this pursuit of green recycling a reality.

A Thank-You to Linda and Affen

I have quickly come to realise that this is not a bad place to live.
Neighbours and friends from all directions have hastened to give,
Love and sustenance in my desolate hour of need,
I know that these gestures of affection will help me to succeed,
In getting through this torment now that Anne has gone.
I must try desperately to find a reason to go on.
I know also that this touching wealth of sentiment,
Is all because of Anne herself and what she meant,
To so many people that she touched with her smile,
I was basking in its glow and all the while,
Hoping that we would be together for many more years,
Why did it have to end in tragedy and tears?
I have at last begun more clearly to see,
One thing that has been so very important to me.
The staunch and instant support of my closest friends,
Linda and Affen whose affection and generosity know no ends.

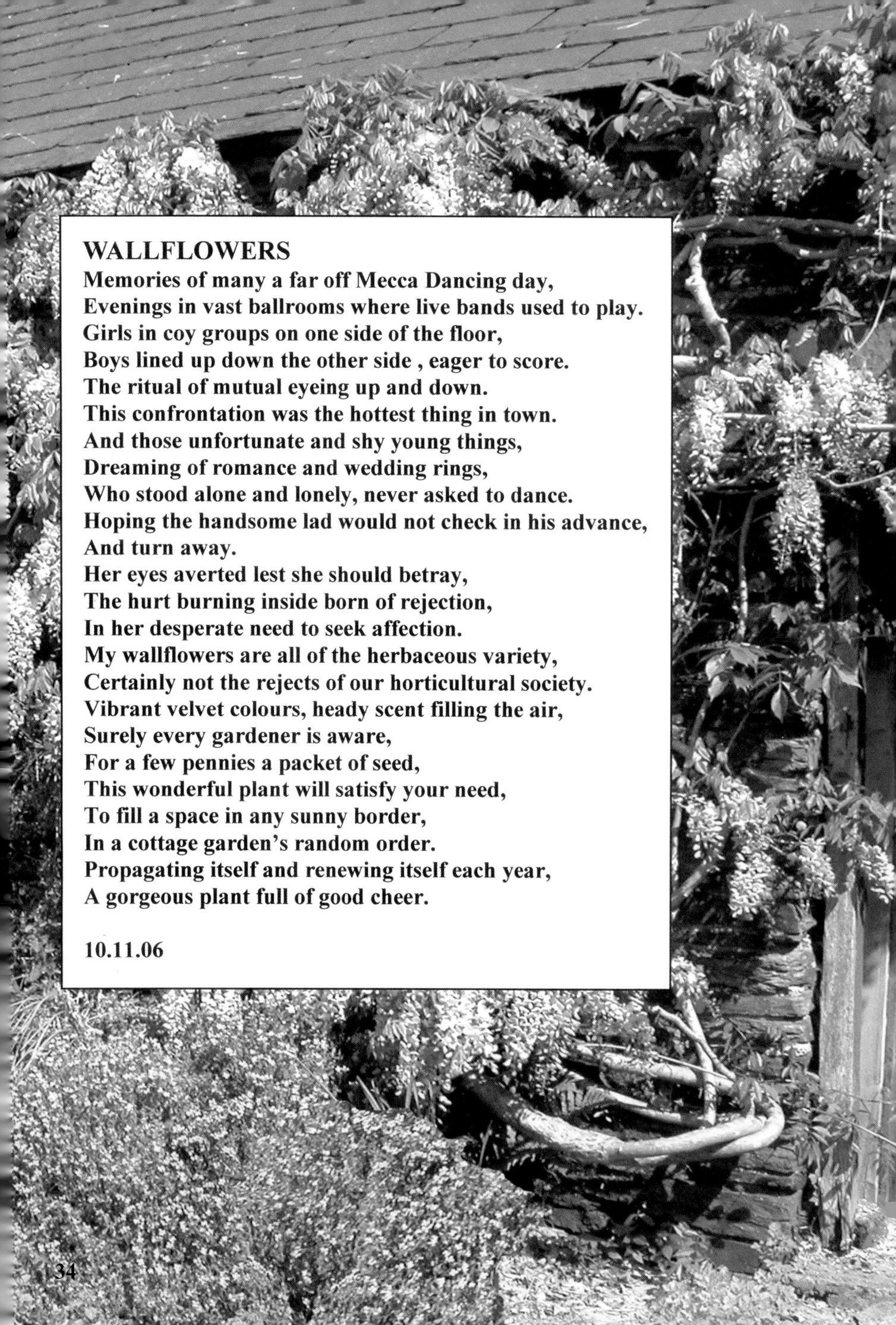

WALLFLOWERS

Memories of many a far off Mecca Dancing day,
Evenings in vast ballrooms where live bands used to play.
Girls in coy groups on one side of the floor,
Boys lined up down the other side , eager to score.
The ritual of mutual eyeing up and down.
This confrontation was the hottest thing in town.
And those unfortunate and shy young things,
Dreaming of romance and wedding rings,
Who stood alone and lonely, never asked to dance.
Hoping the handsome lad would not check in his advance,
And turn away.
Her eyes averted lest she should betray,
The hurt burning inside born of rejection,
In her desperate need to seek affection.
My wallflowers are all of the herbaceous variety,
Certainly not the rejects of our horticultural society.
Vibrant velvet colours, heady scent filling the air,
Surely every gardener is aware,
For a few pennies a packet of seed,
This wonderful plant will satisfy your need,
To fill a space in any sunny border,
In a cottage garden's random order.
Propagating itself and renewing itself each year,
A gorgeous plant full of good cheer.

10.11.06

Mallard

It's April and we have visitors on our lake.
The mallard their reconnaissance to make.
She modest brown, shiny black and green the drake,
protecting her from rivals and the liberties they take.
For three years now they've made their nests,
here as our treasured guests.

This small island she has made her home,
sheltering beneath the weeping willow's dome.
For three weeks she sits the nest in May,
hidden by soft rushes till the day,
her vigil over, she displays her brood,
eleven ducklings search the reeds for food.

Then local predators are here.
Cats from all directions suddenly appear,
attracted by these new arrivals on the scene,
they lie in wait behind the verdant screen.
Ever watchful, the ducks their charges take,
to the centre of the lake.

At first sight of human form, I do believe,
instinctive fear of man tells her to leave.
Despite the dangers lurking round the lake,
she marched her young, escorted by the drake,
off down the hill through bramble patch and meadowsweet,
to the river Siedi they retreat.

Why was it then when visiting Brecon's quay,
at the theatre by the canal, there you could see,
mallard bring their young and motley crew,
to seek the scraps of bread the tourists threw?
No shy birds these but brazen cheek they show,
So different from their country cousins that we know.

29.06.02

The Swan

To Gary and Ann,
Thank you for such a wonderful card,
Knowing you both, you would not find it hard.
Only a photographer and his mate would know where to look,
To understand the skills it took,
To create such an image - a picture so serene,
I wonder at the details in the trees that frame the scene.
Is it symbolic - is that swan me in my isolation?
Or is it Anne - now somewhere in the heaven of creation?
Before I met Anne and came to depend on her embraces,
I used to enjoy the solitude of wild and windy places.
I would seek out some craggy site,
Exposed and blowing with a cold wind's bite,
Where no sketch book could survive,
But in my mind I would derive,
The vital inspiration,
Finely tuned to a deep sensation.
Now that I am alone I will again venture abroad,
Return to that wilderness seeking the reward,
Where I can think unhindered of the Anne I knew,
The deepest love that within me grew,
Ever stronger with each passing day.
Savouring it so sweetly , now that she has gone away.

(For copyright reasons I could not reproduce the original card,
so I painted my own version.)

Reptilian Scales

Last year I had a hip replacement.
They tell you before you get the treatment,
That the prosthesis can break down,
If you are carrying too much weight around.
My recipe for losing weight,
Is to eat off a much smaller plate.
You don't necessarily eat any less than before,
But the size of the plate makes it look like more.
My reaction to these forbidding tales,
Was to buy myself a pair of scales.
I got this ultra-stylish device,
Which had an equally sophisticated price.
All glass plate with the shiny satin metal bit.
An all-singing, all-dancing piece of kit!
I keep it on the bathroom floor,
It sulks in the corner by the door.
There are three little knobs and an LED screen,
Where all the technical data can be seen.
It can cater for a family of up to twenty,
I would have thought that was more than plenty.
You see each person has an individual number of their own,
It can show weight in kilos or by the stone.
You tap the knobs, input height, sex and age,
It's getting too technical for me by this stage.
And by some miracle of modern science,
When you stand on this appliance,
It not only tells you your weight,
Believe me I do not exaggerate,
After the LED flickering, some moments later,
It comes up with this mass of data.
According to this machine, I have no muscle, too much water and too much fat!
Did I pay all this to discover that?

You'd think this masterpiece of modern design,
Would be user friendly and quite benign.
No, I reckon this device is ageist!
It has a built in prejudice.
The minute you put in your age,
You are already beyond the stage,
Where you can trust the infernal machine,
To tell you the truth and to come clean.
This LED screen, all your secrets it betrays.
That little dabble with the Cadbury Milk Trays,
The biscuits and the alcohol banned from your diet,
All those transgressions you wish to keep quiet,
About. Oh I hate this thing!
Although my protestation has a hollow ring.
It's cold, incapable of showing any sympathy.
Why can't it show a greater degree,
Of understanding of my plight.
I'm tempted to drop it from a great height.
To smash the glass, give vent to my hate,
Because it will not fudge my weight.

09.04.08

Dawn

A world observed in silhouette,
When morning light has as yet,
To define a leaf or blade of grass,
A mere matter of allowing time to pass.
Bats glimpsed in their foraging flight,
Tiny pipistrelles, creatures of the night.
A dense chorus of each and every bird,
The sweetest sound you ever heard.
Fills the valley with a thousand songs,
A paradise where my heart belongs.

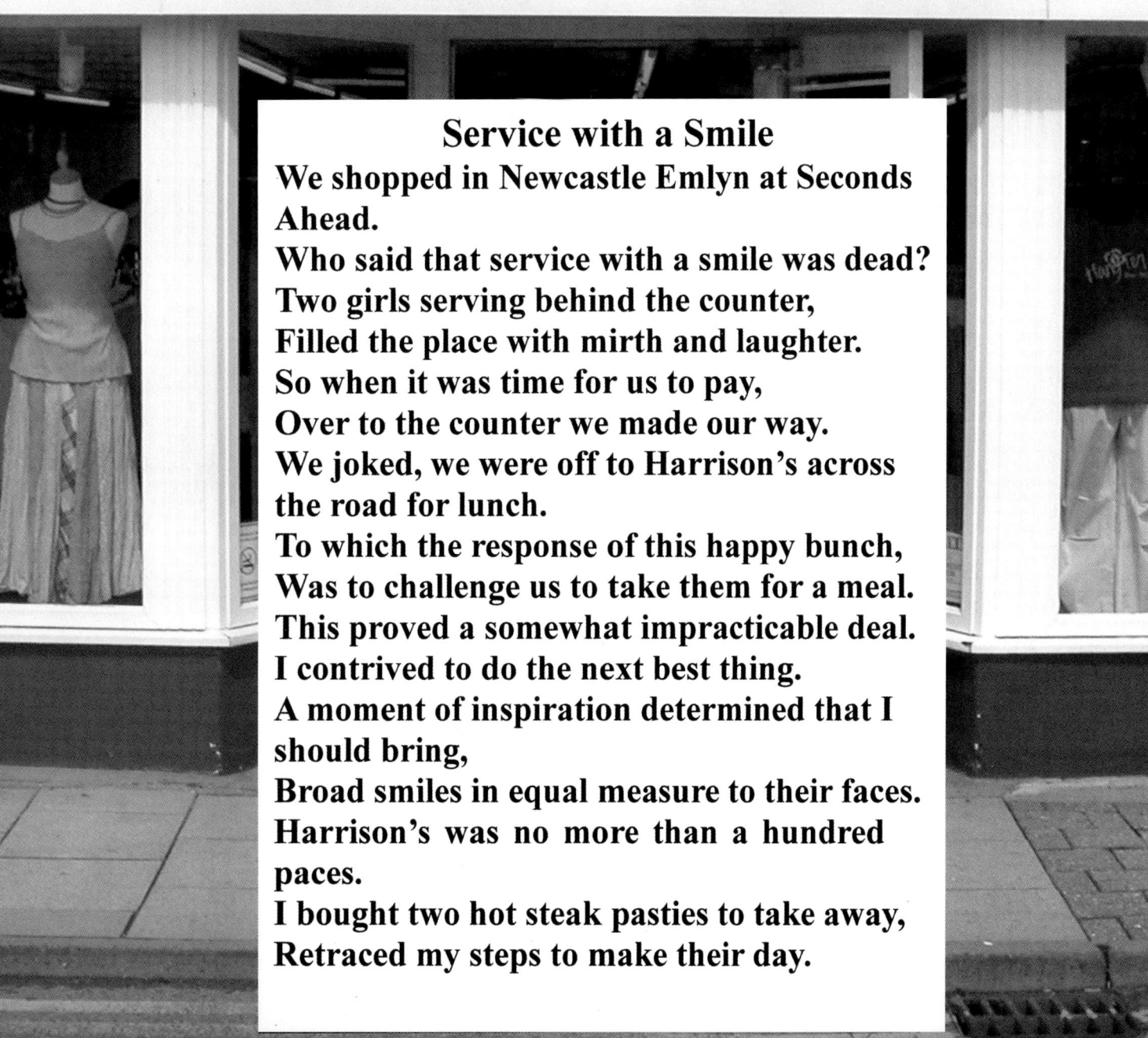

Service with a Smile

We shopped in Newcastle Emlyn at Seconds Ahead.
Who said that service with a smile was dead?
Two girls serving behind the counter,
Filled the place with mirth and laughter.
So when it was time for us to pay,
Over to the counter we made our way.
We joked, we were off to Harrison's across the road for lunch.
To which the response of this happy bunch,
Was to challenge us to take them for a meal.
This proved a somewhat impracticable deal.
I contrived to do the next best thing.
A moment of inspiration determined that I should bring,
Broad smiles in equal measure to their faces.
Harrison's was no more than a hundred paces.
I bought two hot steak pasties to take away,
Retraced my steps to make their day.

The Drunk

I had 12 bottles of whisky in my cellar,
My wife complained I was a drunken feller.
Get rid of each and every one she cried!
I was genuinely traumatized.
I opened the first bottle and poured it down the sink,
Save for one glass I retained for me to drink.
The next bottle I did likewise,
Sampling another glass for size.
The third bottle I did the same.
Barely able to remember my own name.
I pulled the cork from the fourth sink,
And poured the whiskey down the glass to drink.
I drank one sink out of the next bottle and threw the rest down the glass,
Not knowing whether I was on my tits or on my arse!
I pulled the sink out of the next and poured a cork which I drank.
There was whisky all over the floor. The cellar stank.
I corked the sink, bottled the glass and drank the pour.
Had I completed the task? I was not sure.
By now the room began to spin.
Perhaps I should have stuck to gin!
I steadied the house with one hand while I counted out,
The bottles, corks, glasses and sinks strewn all about.
There were 29. To make sure, I counted them all again.
With some difficulty I registered 74 in my brain.
As the house came by I made another count.
Hoping to get a more accurate amount.
Regardless of the number of drinks,
Finally I had all the houses, bottles, corks and sinks,
Except one house and one bottle which I drank.
For this I had my good wife to thank.

20.02.07

This poem is based on an anecdote attributed to Sir Arthur Bryant.

On Desert Island Discs
You are allowed one luxury.
This would be mine...............

A Desert Island Disc

You may wonder why religious music features in an atheists CD collection.
The fact is that church patronage was probably the main source of inspiration.
In an earlier age when atheism was definitely not a wise career move,
Composers had to write pieces that an Archbishop would approve.
If you like early choral works, then Church music it must be.
So I will not admit to any charge of blatant hypocrisy.
Requiems are very common amongst my CD memorabilia,
I wonder is this a serious case of necrophilia?
If I were cast away on some distant speck of sand,
With only a solar powered CD player in my impoverished hand,
This disc of Morten Lauridsen by the singers of Polyphony,
Would make up for the distinct lack of human company.
As their voices echoed through the palm trees, my spirit to enthral,
I could even imagine I was not alone at all.
So a copy of this disc I now bequeath to you,
A magnificent blend of voices for you both to listen to.
06.09.07

A Thank you card to Gary and Ann.

Anne's Legacy
Some people collect stamps and others in search of works of art will go to any ends. Some will collect priceless antiques, but Anne collected friends.
You cannot buy friends and they do not cost a fortune in insurance to secure. Anne's collection was her legacy to me, an estate that will endure.

Be My Valentine

February the Fourteenth is a very special day,
When lovers have the opportunity to say,
To the person of their choice,
Expressed with an amorous tone of voice,
How much they love them, even to implore,
A response from the one that they adore.
Or disclose their intriguing message in a card.
Discovering the sender is never very hard.
Knowing that the subject of one's desires,
Knows exactly who aspires,
To tease and to beguile,
As you attempt to court with style,
Declaring in words of deep emotion,
Vows of your everlasting devotion.
Making an impassioned plea,
'Will you be the one for me?'

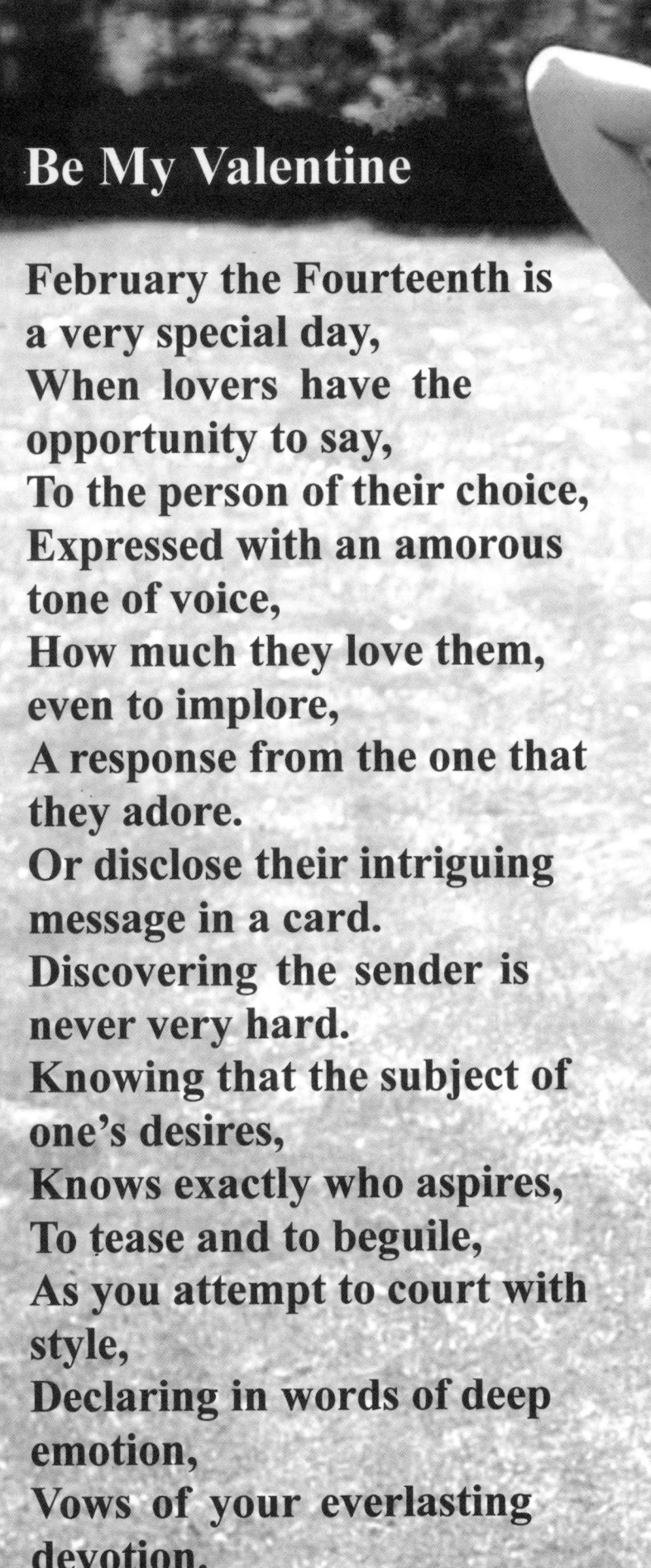

Fishing

I had a call from Rob today,
To ask if he and Eleri could pay,
A visit to my pond to fish.
It was Eleri's dearest wish,
To catch some wildlife for her tank.
What fairy of chance had I to thank?
For the delight of having them to tea,
Providing another opportunity.
For me to meet this cute young child.
Everyone who meets her is beguiled,
By her chubby smile, the button nose,
The fine blonde tresses and the kiddies clothes.
Of course, Bramble had to come as well.
I am still under this Jack Russell's spell.
I find calm and a sense so utterly serene,
When such dear friends as these have been,
To bring great pleasure to my day.
Another sweet memory tucked away,
In the inner sanctum of my mind,
Which in years to come I will seek to find,
When this young girl has come of age,
And looks on me as some wizened sage.
No matter, I hope I live that long,
And that her love for her father, stays true and strong.

06.04.08

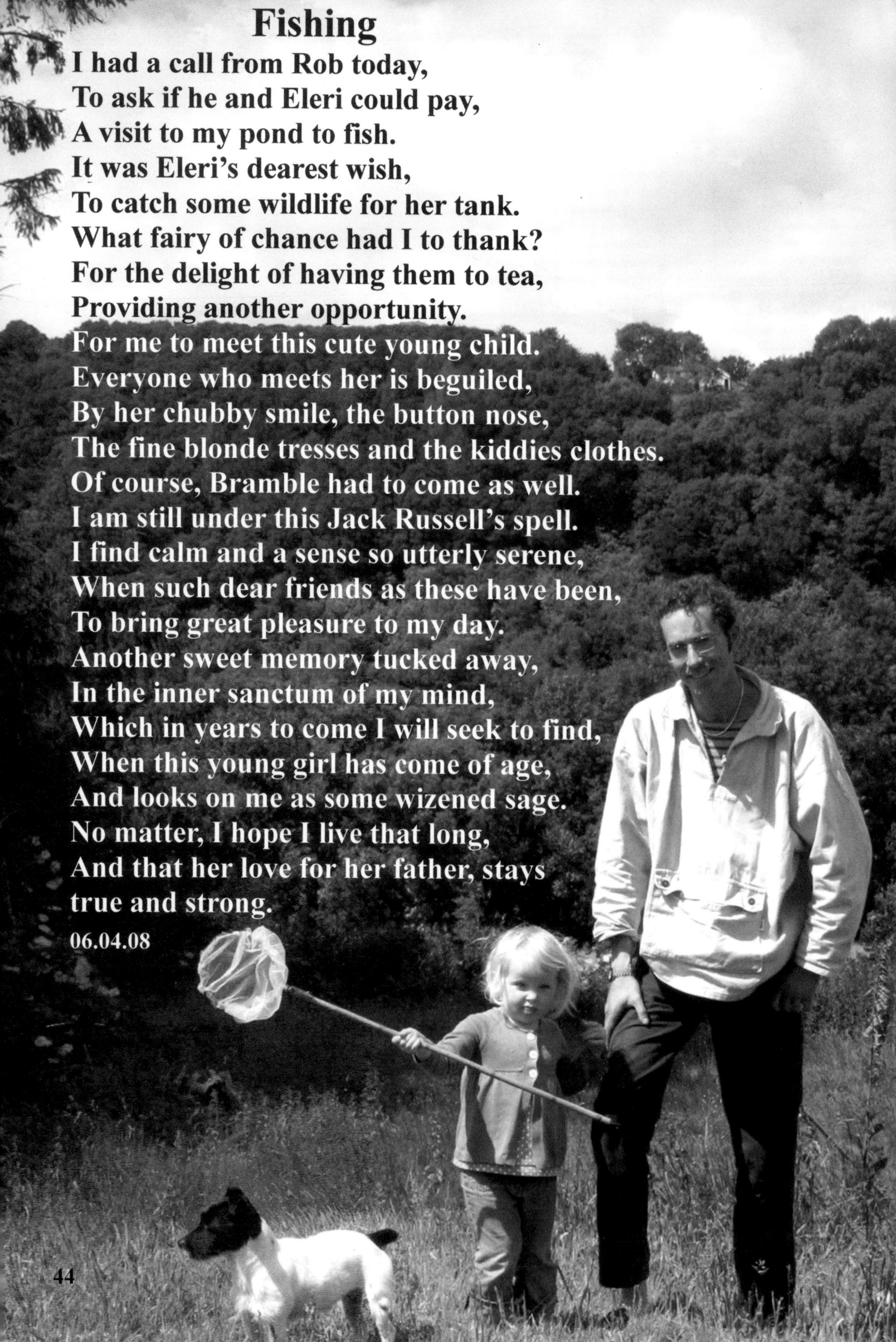

Sex and the Colour Green

I have to admit that my wife Anne was not the first Welsh girl that I had a lustful crush on.
When I was a horrid and despicable, twelve year old moron,
It was during the early years at my Grammar School,
There was at least one lesson in which I did not fool,
Around. It was Mathematics taken by the delectable Miss Morgan,
That caused the first stirrings in my diminutive sexual organ.
She used to wear a green corduroy suit with a short pencil skirt,
On reflection, she was probably an outrageous flirt.
This was the secret of her fascination and the completeness of her control.
And of course her red hair, her Welsh temper and dark eyes that pierced ones very soul.
Green fishnet stockings clad shapely legs which she crossed and uncrossed with alarming frequency,
Tantalisingly perched on the edge of the desk, right in front of me.
Long before Sharon Stone and that infamous scene in Fatal Attraction,
Long before the notorious film director called Camera and Action!
Then there was Ingrid a sexy foreign student who came to stay.
My sister was studying German, exchanges of this type were the new order of the day.
On sunny summer afternoons we'd play lengthy games of tennis,
She used to wear a ridiculously, short and revealing white dress.
Ah! Those flashing glimpses of shiny satin knickers in a subtle shade of turquoise green.
Don't be too judgemental, I had only just turned thirteen.
I suppose the colour was turquoise, although there was certainly more green than blue.
However I will leave all the psychoanalysis to you.
And when Anne and I finally made it to the altar,
She wore a divine dark green suit with a soft mink collar.
A matching fur hat that was perched seductively on her head.
Can you blame me that I could not wait to get her into bed!

The Cellar Bar

The Cellar Bar in Cardigan - a magical place secreted underground,
Where people who love poetry rally to the sound,
Of the spoken word expressed in rhyme,
What better way to while away the time.
Together, Steve and April have created this intimate place,
Where you and I come face to face.
Mutually drawn here to perform,
Collectively working up the 'perfect storm'.
My first time here I was amazed!
Would this lot be hyper-intellectual and half crazed?
Would it be arty-farty, excruciatingly formal?
To look at you - you seem quite normal.
But that is clearly not the case.
The fantastic use of words - the subtle grace,
Of poems read aloud performed on stage,
So much more telling than silent reading from a page.
Sue and Simone set the scene,
Brilliant wit on a scientific theme.
Just follow That!
Inevitably my virgin name was first out of the hat!
I loved hearing all your work - its intriguing variety,
The humour, depth of feeling, insight - the sheer diversity.
So many magic moments to savour, my senses and heart to please.
I thank you for your cordial welcome, you made me feel so much at ease.
I know this sounds utterly absurd,
But I only came here to pull a bird!

Maggie Harris on stage

Pick-Up Line

It saddens me, my poetry makes you cry,
May I be the one to caress the tear drop from the corner of your eye?
04.04.08

Cellar Bar Girl

Dear Steve and April,
You really have created something very special here,
Last night was an occasion that brought great cheer,
To a sad, old gentleman like me,
As desperate as any desperate man could be!
I have long been an observer of the human condition.
There is, of course, always the suspicion,
That this voyeuristic tendency,
Conceals a serious case of impotency.
In a Cellar Bar packed with beautiful people - one stood out.
This is what people-watching is all about.
Do gentlemen really prefer blondes? Let us not forget,
The awesome power of a ravishing brunette!
Tall with a cascade of raven black hair,
Radiating such an imperious air,
I simply could not turn my eyes away,
I could have watched this creature forever and a day.
This lady - looking particularly cute,
Dressed in a stone-washed denim suit.
Normally denim would not be my choice by any means,
But the way this girl filled a pair of jeans,
Forced me immediately to change my mind.
A born-again experience of the shattering kind!
Who she was will remain a mystery.
That I lacked the courage to approach her sadly I must agree.
A simple confession I have to say,
But seeing such a vision really made my day!

18.05.08

Respect

Respect is observing the speed limit when driving through town.
Respect is turning the volume on your ghetto blaster down.
Not lighting a bonfire when your neighbour's washing's on the line.
Placing you litter in a bin rather than incur a fine.

Respect is opening doors to help people on their way.
Making polite conversation to pass the time of day.
Giving up your seat to a pensioner on a crowded train or bus.
Sorting out problems with diplomacy, without a fuss.

Respect is doing as Romans do when you are in Rome.
Taking muddy shoes off when entering someone else's home.
Making yourself scarce when your daughter's boyfriend's in the lounge.
Being generous when a mate is on the scrounge.

Respect is giving away the last toffee with a purple wrapper.
Respect is refraining from calling mother-in-law and old slapper.
Telling her she looks amazing when you know it is not true.
Doing unto others as you would have them do to you.

Wouldn't life be so much more wonderful if we all contrived,
Not open the Champagne until the guest of honour has arrived.
Not to stick chewing gum where it might embarrass or offend.
Not to do those things that drive parents round the bend.

The moral of this story is take time to think of others.
Look the other way when confronted by breast-feeding mothers.
Be the one to answer telephone calls in the middle of the night.
Accept the sobering fact that you are not always right.

Pain

Pain comes in many forms and infinite variety.
The subtle hurt of violation of one's piety.
The mental anguish that is impossible to grasp,
Tears at the fabric of your soul as if a metal rasp.
When the physical hurt of sudden brutal impact hits.
The fear of those prone to uncontrolled and violent fits.

The relentless dull ache of some internal disorder,
That eats away one's resolution even to the border,
Of insanity! Can someone make this stop!
Such pain can drain resistance to the very last drop.
There's nothing left. Nowhere to turn.
Nothing can stem its fire's all consuming burn.

The pain of loss. Of loved ones. That loyal devoted pet.
The desolation of returning from that final visit to the Vet.
No more wet muzzle or the welcome of a wagging tail.
Did you delay the inevitable for some selfish end or fail,
To face up to the reality we do not wish to know,
That it was far kinder to just let go.

In childbirth pain is combined with joy.
No matter that the baby is a girl or boy.
Whether labour is lengthy or quite natural,
Assisted by caesarian section or an epidural.
All is forgotten when the baby's first cry breaks the tension.
Parenthood brings to life a new dimension.

For some pain is the ultimate, exquisite pleasure,
Sought out in the most extreme pursuit of leisure.
The scourge, the tightened strap or bondage chain.
Endorphins sent surging through the blood stream to the brain.
The ultimate fix, for that drug-like addiction,
Submissive to Miss Whiplash's domination.

All pain is of course relative,
Not always cured by sedative.
A clumsy carpenter who hammers his thumb,
Knows a blow to a second digit, renders the other numb.
Messages to the brain get thoroughly confused,
When flesh is so seriously abused.

Then there is the pain that can be caused by laughter.
Splitting one's sides, torn uncontrollably after,
An hilarious joke, or someone falling flat on their face.
Unless you are that person whose fall from grace,
Leaves them the object of public ridicule.
People can be so very cruel.

A Poem for this Day

I thought I ought to write something today for today.
Not necessarily a poem - a recitation you might say.
I was up ay 4 this morning not unlike a year ago,
When I wrote another poem about the scene below.

Wild ragged clouds in slow motion drifted across the skies,
In them the ride of the Valkyrie I could visualize.
Or was it a more threatening apocalyptic omen?
Was it a vision of the four, fearsome horsemen?

No wind in the trees, bats still chasing insects in erratic flight ,
The dawn chorus had not started, it was not completely light.
The odd cockerel and bleating lambs across the valley,
And underlying this the bubbling sounds of the river Siedi.

I remembered when we lived in Edgware at such an hour,
It was impossible to escape the M1's distant roar.
Even when cast away on Bora Bora's tropic shore,
Waves crashing on coral reefs, no true silence anymore.

Escaping the towns and all the bustle and the bother,
We merely exchange one set of sounds and smells for another.
Savour the freshness and variety compared to the cities,
We must accept each environment for what it is.

By now the odd car passing through the village, speeding on its way,
The first bird to sing, a chiff-chaff, how tiring doing that all day.
A heron flew in and on the old blasted oak he found a perch.
On seeing me, off he went some other pond to search.

Dawn brought a shepherd's warning of the reddest kind,
Childhood memories of wartime suddenly sprang to mind.
Looking south to London, incendiary fires raging through the night,
Colouring the cloud and smoke above the city, set the sky alight.

Wisps of pale yellow cirrus swirled with feathered grace,
Choreographed like a distant ballet staged on the edge of space.
Now the dawn chorus and the rustle of a breeze
Sunbeams bursting through the branches of the trees.

Then the crash bang of the dustmen, busy on their round,
And suddenly I realised I could no longer hear the sound,
Of the river Siedi babbling on its way,
Now swallowed up in the noise and bustle of the day.

04.09.03

A Universal Vision

Where I live in Wales the Milky Way can still be seen at night,
Yet to fall victim to the insidious creep of sodium light.
This cosmic highway of glistening dust, meanders across the sky,
Even man's puny satellites can be followed with the naked eye.

Stonehenge stands a monument to the skills of ancient man,
In marking patterns of the seasons before recorded history began.
The pyramids bear witness to the early mastery of mathematics,
The powerful influence of astronomy on religion and politics.

As we venture ever further into the depths of space,
If we do find intelligent life, will it have a human face?
Can the mysteries of Titan reveal the origins of life on Earth?
Can scientists really calculate the moment of our planet's birth?

Now we are no longer earthbound in our universal observation,
Images from the Hubble telescope offer amazing inspiration,
Stirring interest in Science amongst the younger generation,
To seek solutions to these questions with eager anticipation.

20.01.05

On the Way to Somewhere Else

At night a canopy of stars, no light pollution here.
Ursa Major and Cassiopeia, Their celestial realm is clear.
Yet satellites observing like some alien force,
Mere specks of dust, the eye can trace their course.

Cold cauldron, its swirling vapours rise,
To join the mists that veil the skies,
Now tinged with pink to greet the sun,
Night steals away, the day's begun.

Overhead a glint of continental flight,
Intruding on the early morning light.
Is there nowhere in this world that's free,
From all pervading eyes to see.

I will conjure you a thousand shades of green.
Oak, willow and alder, city folks have rarely seen.
A dawn chorus to celebrate the coming of the day.
An avian orchestra for your delight to play.

Forget your paranoia, be like the Welsh.
All travellers are on the way to somewhere else.
They have no concept of our quality of life.
Let them concern themselves with stress and strife.

Those motorists escaping cities, one assumes,
Who sit in weekend traffic fuelled by fumes,
Seeking an elusive goal beyond their reach,
To join the masses already crowded on the beach.

Happy is he who can create a space,
That is for him a very special place.
No need to fly to foreign parts to get away,
This is both home and where he wants to stay.

29.06.02

Introspection

I make no great claim to work of any intellectual moment,
I paint a picture, tell a story with uncomplicated content.
Usually with a moral or a message to give point to the verse,
Fearful of academic criticism, thoughts of a humiliating reverse.
Baffled by those who decried the works of Dylan Thomas,
That they should take my untutored efforts into their withering focus.

I have no literary pedigree, I cannot claim to be well read,
I have not spent hours of study, analysing what other poets said.
Not sure of my metre, more concerned with how it sounds.
Not even confident that I should have the grounds,
To even call myself a poet. What audacity to make such a claim.
Despite any such doubts, I will carry on regardless just the same.

Poetry and pictures set to music and presented on DVD.
This versatile new medium, offered such opportunities to me.
The potential of the desktop computer made me appreciative,
How modern technology has opened up new ways to be creative.
What would Virgil and Catullus have made of these facilities,
To hone, polish and express their exceptional abilities.

04.06.04

The River Siedi

The River Siedi*, over rocks and pebbles, takes its course,
To join the Teifi* no more than four miles from its source.
Host to dipper and kingfisher, trout and salmon come here to spawn.
In shallow pools their eggs to lay and die before another dawn.

It may not have the greatest river's length,
At times a raging torrent shows its strength.
Any naturalist should realise the part it has to play,
Make it his duty, its vital role portray.

Its constant waters fuelled the mills,
Where woollen weavers once applied their skills,
At Derw and Henfryn they plied their trade,
Cloth and blankets of fine quality were made.

A shaded pool, the shafts of sunlight penetrate,
Deep in the water's pebbled depth to concentrate,
The eye on ghostly shapes that ride the currents flow,
Silver phantoms darting to and fro.

At first it seems no fish are there,
Just stones and water greet one's stare,
Time passing focuses the eye on subtle camouflage,
Detecting their movement, a shimmering mirage.

Once, while browsing in the National Gallery,
One picture, all dots and random colours, fascinated me,
I studied it from near and far the subject to find out,
First eye then fin and tail. It was a trout.

What had been just diffuse colour in disarray,
The artist with skill his tricks to play,
Challenging the eye its identity concealed.
Suddenly the features of his subject in clear order were revealed.

And so it is in nature we fail to see so many things.
Not taking the time to seek the clarity that contemplation brings.
So sit awhile, enjoy the countryside and meditate.
The colour form and changing light appreciate.

* Siedi is pronounced 'Sheddy', and Teifi as 'Tie-vee'.

The Heron

Grey and White, crested with plumes of black,
This large bird in loping flight, with neck drawn back,
Long legs trailing, it glides across the sky,
Scanning the ground below for any water that is nearby.

They say that herons will never encroach,
On the hunting ground of others as they watch,
Sharp-eyed and with even sharper beak,
Poised, motionless to catch the unsuspecting fish they seek,

Just place a model heron by your pond.
This will protect the fish of which you are so fond.
How foolish to believe such an old wives' tale,
Many have tried this defence to no avail.

Herons often visit us in threes.
At dusk they come to roost in the taller trees,
Beside the water. Then at first light,
They descend to plunder every fish in sight.

To stop a heron some allege,
Maintain a cordon at the waters edge.
This provision, they assure, will not allow,
The bird to wade in where the pond is shallow.

To a certain extent this statement is true,
But it disregarded what the heron knew,
That he could land directly in the shallow water,
To him this barrier was such a trivial matter.

In the three years since I stocked the pond with fish,
It was always my fervent wish,
That they would spawn and increase the stock,
In defiance of the heron flock.

And so it is, a natural balance has been achieved,
The fish survive in numbers as I believed.
Heron and kingfisher come to take their share,
However, I still leave the defences there!

28.01.03

The Psychiatrists Chair

I had gone to speak to Roger Spencer,
Who runs the Trefheddyn Garden Centre.
There I had this brief encounter,
With an attractive lady who was about to enter.
I almost collided with her as I stopped,
To retrieve the umbrella she had dropped.
So I returned to the salon for the appointment I had just booked.
And while seated, waited as I looked,
Who was to walk in but the lady I had just met.
Surely she did not need a shampoo and set.
Why should she wish to titivate,
Her hair, already quite immaculate.
I soon understood why she was there,
As she, Angie, sat me in the chair,
And proceeded to part and cut my hair.
It is amazing the secrets you reveal,
Express openly the way you feel,
When looking at the reflection in the mirrors,
Of your hair dresser, deftly wielding her pair of scissors.
Observing the skills of this strawberry blonde,
Transforming your hair as if waving a magic wand.
It seems you are completely without concern,
That the ears of those awaiting their turn,
Might ever so slightly start to burn,
As they anticipate what they may soon learn,
Eagerly hoping to hear the beans you are about to spill.
With a NATO standard coffee perched on the sill,
Which leaves you thoroughly relaxed,
Contemplating the pile of hair that has just been axed.

Poem   The White Vans

Over thirty years ago, at RAF Hendon I used to teach,
That the power of the computer would bring within our reach,
A time when the rush hour, the commuter's daily grind,
Would be a thing of the past, left far behind.
Working from home, linked by the fastest communications,
Modern businesses would conduct their operations,
Their staff dispersed across the land, far and wide,
Living healthier lives, deep in the countryside.

A computer terminal in the workplace was new and strange,
It was my task to overcome their resistance to change,
Explain how new technology would affect their working lives,
Emphasise the many diverse benefits that society derives,
From such advances - put stress on the positive side,
Counter comments from the 'Luddites' that would deride,
The 'little green screens' enslaving the working population,
Creating a race of square-eyed zombies throughout the nation.

Man had recently set foot upon the Moon.
Surely, one concluded, it was inevitable that soon,
There would be satellite industries operating there,
Taking advantage of the lack of atmosphere.
Well, as yet, such predictions have not come to pass.
Not all technological advances have brought benefit, alas.
Despite congestion charges, the rush hour still exists,
Man's ingrained herding instinct still persists.

The situation, however, is not all one of doom and gloom,
Those of us escaping to the country have enjoyed a boom,
Spawned by the Internet, broadband and the mobile phone,
However isolated and remote, we are not alone,
Whether ordered from catalogue or website, never mind,
There is no spot the ubiquitous transit van cannot find.
The blur of white - rushing helter-skelter down country lanes,
Bringing sustaining life blood to our extremities' veins.

14.09.04

Anne's Father Jack

Jack Pullen

The first thing Anne's father
said to me was 'You're a toff!'
I smiled and tried to laugh it off.
Not the best of beginnings I'm afraid,
But Anne as usual came to my aid,
And matters were easily resolved,
And a strong friendship soon evolved.
There was about him a rugged, under-stated style.
After all he played professional football for Plymouth Argyll,
Had International caps for Wales,
A centre half as hard as nails.
In truth, he was a gentle man.
His sporting career had a fifteen year span,
Eventually ended by serious injury.
He returned to Ebbw Vale to work for RTB,
In the huge steel works which once filled the valley,
Now long closed down. Consigned to history.
He was a man of considerable achievements, not brash and loud,
With a son and daughter of whom he was immensely proud.
Straightforward, never guilty of doing anything for effect.
He was a gentleman who commanded everyone's respect.

21.08.06

Global Village
I ponder the paths that brought me to this place,
Revealed in the lines and furrows etched into my weathered face.
Proud of my family, devoted to my lovely wife,
Those crucial decisions that shaped the pattern of my life.

Was I ever suited to a military career?
The Junior Entry Lines were brutal and severe.
The crowing and rigid discipline of that Cranwell 'garrison',
A Battle-School that made any boot camp tame in comparison!

Despite the trauma of that arduous initiation,
A youthful resolve to face that situation,
Hardened my capacity to undertake the challenges ahead,
Following wherever the footprint of fate had lead.

Friendships and loyalty forged there that have endured,
Deep in one's subconscious mind, indelibly secured.
A military life severs contact with familiar ground.
Bereft of any roots, posted and randomly moved around.

A global village of friends and neighbours scattered far and wide.
Always the newcomers where you eventually reside.
Though contact is broken - addresses lost or left behind,
That bond remains within the inner reaches of your mind.

26.02.07

Age Concern Extreme Make Over
I'm still at the stage where I want to live forever,
On second thoughts that might not seem so clever.
It's OK if every faculty is still in place,
It's not just about jazzing up one's face.
I conduct my life with the energy of a much younger man,
I work for the community and do as much as I can,
 And use my experience for their benefit.
I genuinely feel that I am pretty fit.
I must admit officials no longer ask for proof I'm an OAP,
It certainly does not feel that I am seventy to me.
The time is coming when we will be fitted with spare parts,
When Medical Science has honed its stem cell arts.
Check in for a service. Get your personal MOT.
It all sounds extraordinarily far-fetched to me.
What if I got rid of those wrinkles with a brow lift and a tuck,
No! It would fool nobody – I don't have that sort of luck.
I suppose I might benefit from extensive liposuction,
I might even dabble with some tidy breast augmentation!
Teeth. OK. Pity about the hair,
Do I really want an implanted 'barnet' bristling up there?
Do I really want my facial skin stretched so tight?
The muscles seem frozen. I can't get my words out right.
I could finish up with keloid scars the colour of tomato sauce!
In the end it's probably wiser to let life take its course.
08.04.08

Quality of Life
Cry not for us, as pensioners we do not seek your pity,
That our joint annual income is but a tenth of some twenty something working in the city.
Our Christmas bonus is a government fuel supplement,
Hardly comparable to that of a young city gent!
We find that we can live quite comfortably within our means,
No need for bejewelled Dior gowns or designer jeans,
To feature in our long term strategy, our scheme of things,
That such a materialistic craving inevitably brings.
Some time ago we escaped from that city strife.
We are now blessed with a far better quality of life.
Some people might consider us to be ranked amongst the poor,
We find no pressing need to keep up with them next door.
We now live happily amongst all the Jones's in West Wales,
Boosted by the occasional visit to the January sales.

22.08.07
PS
I fear for these young people destined to burn out,
When markets are in free-fall, like headless chickens run about,
A crisis caused by injudicious mortgage lending,
Allied to the failure of attempts at creative accounting.
Paid these large sums for speculation with other peoples money,
Buzzing greedily like wasps round a pot of honey.
They claim that they can only take the pressure for a few years,
Before it finally gets to them and they depart in tears.
Of course in that time they have amassed a considerable fortune.
To retreat like us would now seem to be most opportune.

A Cat Called Angharad

I met a cat today, Angharad was her name,
Known as Haddy for short, she ignored me just the same,
Eighteen years old and obviously very wise,
Petite and regal of manner from which one might surmise,
That in her lifetime she has seen a thing or two,
She utters a most royal meow to summon you.
I picked her up and fondled her, she did not object.
Surely, is this not the affection such a beauty would expext?
I envy David and Tara their precious bond,
With this lovely creature of whom they are so fond.
That she should trespass in to the public domain,
Was my good fortune - a memory I will treasure and retain.

02.06.06

A thank-you to David and Tara - Morgan's Brasserie, St Davids.

The Beauties of Aberystwyth

Now that I am old and widowed I must remember to behave.
There is one luxury that I admit I crave,
This indulgence to you I now reveal,
I love to go to Aberystwyth for a meal.
I had gone there to celebrate,
Handing to Cambrian Printers all the material to create,
This book of poetry dedicated to my late wife,
Such a lovely girl - the love of my life.
I enjoy the wholesome food,
And the House Red is particularly good,
In the Carvery by the Promenade,
Though I really find it extremely hard,
So extraordinarily difficult to understand,
That there should be so many beautiful girls with no rings on the third fingers of their left hand!
They wait at tables in this Restaurant,
What better service could a red blooded male want!
What is wrong with the men of Aberystwyth?
Am I missing something or is it obviously no myth,
That the chaps up here have only one thing on their mind,
An all-consuming passion of the Rugby Football kind.
I must confess this fundamental torment lingers,
To see the appalling nakedness of these delectable ring fingers!
This dilemma I have pondered deep and long,
A s to how I could right this grievous wrong.
Now that I am available and fancy free,
It suddenly occurred to me,
If I may venture to be so bold,
In order to clothe their nakedness with bands of gold,
They allow me to realise my fantasy,
That they all agree to marry me!

04.07.08